Opening Night
The Christmas Poems

MARK GREENE

2 MARTIN
RRREAT SALESMAN !
OCH JOY
DGREENE
RISTMAS '95

This book is dedicated to
Maurice and Jean Greene, my parents,
and still admitting it after all these years.
With much love.

CONTENTS

The Offer

It was an offer
She could have refused,
A life she could have used
In some other way.
To grow great with child, for example,
After her wedding day;
To forego the knowing looks
And the slur of slut;
To defer to another the chance to tell a father
And watch the word twist in her fiancé's gut;
To make room for some noble's daughter
To carry the cause of innocents' slaughter;
To allow some other to cradle a son
Pale from his pinioned death.

She could have said:
'All things considered,
And though I am flattered,
I would rather not.
I am just a village girl,
Not fit for such matters.'

Of course, there was the sigh of angel's wings,
The words with all his promises ripened for now,
The chance to do something extraordinary,
To let what was ordinary become...
But afterwards would it not all seem such girlish fancy?

She, turning from the safety
Of merely human possibility,
Marvelling at how could it be,
That he should choose her to bless,
Welcomed truth to her womb, and said 'yes'.

The Trip

It was not doubt
That took her on the road.
The angel's words did not fade
With the passing of days .
No, it was not doubt
That made her exclaim
The question the sceptics
Would pose again and again:
'How can it be, and I a virgin still?'
Not doubt, more like an amazed joy
That soared above the shout of shame.

It was not doubt,
That took her to the hills,
More like a zealous curiosity
To see for herself
How he was working it out,
To skip in the track of each new step,
To laugh at the mound of evidence,
Elizabeth's baby swelling her dress,
Confounding the critics' common sense:
'How can it be, and she beyond the age?'
To learn that the child leapt in the womb
Just at their presence in the room.

To hear, from someone she could trust,
Who knew that hers was not the bloom
Of some undiscovered, earthy lust,
That through her labour would come rest,
Mercy after such insistence at the breast,
Heaven from this tiny, terrestrial guest.

How can it be, how can it be.

Gravity

The apple, unlike Adam, had no choice but to fall,
Speeding to fulfil its creator's call.
But what force drew him down to us?
He, with a starlit infinity to explore,
He, who could peer into a neutron's core,
He, who had spoken a thousand million times
And known the sulphuric spit of our self-vaunting
    crimes,
He, whom we had called murderer, liar, thief
And left for dead with enlightened relief.

What force drew him down from above
To reap the grim harvest of rebel pride,
Hammered with nails of truth denied?
What force drew him down from above?
What force but this: the gravity of love.

One Move Ahead

Probably he wouldn't have otherwise,
He, a good man, and his girl
Defiled, it seemed, by another man's smile.
But the voice in the dream
Sharp and sure
Like the words in the scroll
Told a different story:
She is pure, she is pure.

Probably he wouldn't have gone otherwise,
He, a good man, and his bride
Eight months or so with child.
Not that far, at least.
Two weeks along the cold, uneven road,
The donkey bumping and jerking its bulging load.

But great Caesar Augustus,
For reasons of his own,
He supposed, chose this time
To number the mortals
Under his divine throne,
Sending each to register
In their natal home.

So they went.
Perhaps for a while surprised
That the Almighty should require
Such discomfort of his chosen.

But along the cold, uneven road,
Pondering an angel's words,
She, whose humility conceived a king in her womb,
Perhaps did not worry that the journey
Would bring the child too soon.
And he, whose will had been overturned by a dream,
Must have marvelled at the elegance of the divine
    scheme:
The Lord who had trumped the imperial decree
Would wait til they came to the appointed place:
Son of Joseph in Joseph's town
Son of David come for his crown.

Probably he wouldn't have gone otherwise,
He, a good father, and his wife
So recently a mother,
And the child so small,
When the voice came again:
And this of blood on Herod's mind.

But the starmen had been and left
Gold, frankincense and myrrh,
Portable gifts, easily turned to food and shelter,
And were they not fully equipped
And the distance already half done
For the desert road down,
Down, down to alien Egypt.

He, they realised, was always one move ahead.

Travelling Light

It wasn't much to go on,
You might say,
Obvious enough to the naked eye
But still just one more glimmer
In a glimmering sky.
A clue easily overlooked,
A sign easily passed by
In the bustle of familiar days.

So, they, alone of all those who saw, set out,
Leaving behind friends who must have thought them
    mad:
This time, this time they were going too far,
Just a tad too intense about the rightness of their view;
And families fearing for their lives
On a long journey to who knew where.
Certainly they didn't,
Having no book to say it was this, then and there.

So they, alone in all the world, set out.
A relief it must have been just to be going and gone...

Almost at the end, up to a king's court,
Seeking some answer to their destination,
His wise men told them precisely where:
Just a few miles down the road.
But the wise did not care
To join them.
Of course, they had seen the star
And the book had told them just where,
But five miles, five miles is just a tad too far.

So, as at the start, alone, persuading no one along the
    way,
They, who had left friends, family and sanity behind,
To find: a few animals, a man and his wife, and in the
    hay,
A child who had no words to say, no gifts to bestow,
No way to show his pleasure at their adoration,
They did not exult that yes,
Yes, all along they had been right
But bowed down, for here,
Here, at last was the light.

Opening Night

A spotlight locked on a small provincial town.
A shed converted for the purpose.
The steamy breath of animals,
Shuffling at a teenager's cries.
And finally,
A different cry, the sweat mopped away.
The quiet.
The crunch of straw pressed down.
Her child asleep.

Not many came,
Though this was where they said it would be.
A few out-of-towners from the east,
A handful of nightworkers on the skive.
Not many came
To see this ordinary sight,
The new Life lit by a singular light.

Out of the Blue...

The historic present.

And future perfect
Concentrated in him
Infinite love locked in linen.

The answer,

To purpose,
and the ache of the heart
and the clench of the knotted will,

Poised to pour
Fulness
Cascading
Beyond the brim of all we are

The king
Laying his gifts at our feet.

What Herod Knew

He,
Who had already killed a brother,
A wife, a son and then another,
And then another,
And found a certain peace,
He knew the dread power
Of an idea to wrench
The mind from ordinary ways.

But the travellers,
With a star in their eye
And their tale of a king,
He thought quaint,
Sending them south to the predicted place,
And waiting for their disappointed return.
Then long year long he pondered their absence,
Knowing that seekers may make truth of concidence.

He knew
A child will grow;
That innocence may turn to threat;
That hope may storm
The empire of the heart;
That the wind may blow
A seed to a hilltop death.

He knew.
And just to make sure
Suffered the little innocents
Spiked on his rebel crown,
And found a certain peace.

He knew.
And would rather have killed him in the womb.
We, too late for that, and with no taste for blood,
Would simply drown the rumour of an empty tomb.

Kings

We were not three.
And not kings.
At least not when we arrived.
And really more curious than wise,
Craning for truth in starlit skies.
But at least looking,
At least checking
What we thought we knew:
A king born for the Jews.

No, we were not wise.
More stupid than wise,
Asking another king
To point us to a rival's cradle.
But at least asking,
And finding truth in the old scroll,
Truth a murderer would not recognise,
But wary still to ply us with winsome lies
And play a deferential role.

No, we were not so wise.
More blind than wise,
Searching for a king
For someone else.
But at least searching,
And finding, in someone else's king,
Our end, the end of lifeless ways,
The rule for all our days.

Later they fancied us kings.
In that, there was only this truth:
He who would wear a crown
Must first bow low,
Must first bow down.

White Christmas

Some dreams may come true:
>Chestnuts roasting on an open fire,
>The soothing cool of mediterranean blue,
>The rustling shimmer of wedding white.

The old seer's dream,
His eye scoured of fanciful self-delusion,
Saw this:

>A cedar hacked to a stump,
>Springing a new shoot;

>The village virgin's impossible boy
>Crowned universal king;

>The innocent prince pinned
>Against the protesting sky
>By the dark insistent lie
>Of his adulterous bride.

This dream,
Sure in its renewed proposal,
      The eternal breeze whispering our name,
      The desert heart fountaining with joy,

This dream,
      Real in her expectant womb,
      Real in the blooded planks of that severed tree
      And the blast-bright fulness of his empty tomb,

This dream

Came true.

Simeon

Of a morning
The ancient breeze would unfurl,
Gentle on the old man.
Together they would go
To the place of promise.

And promise had been made,
Nested in his heart,
And promise had lain there,
Content for the future.
Only occasionally, as the years blew by,
Gusted by anxiety, he would wonder:
'Will he be, will he be?'

On this day,
The breeze, fresh and damp,
A herald of summer rain,
Nipped his heels and scurried him on
To the customary place,
His legs aching by strange compulsion
His eye seeking some horizon...

A man, a pair of pigeons, a woman,
                    And a baby.

Promise soared,
A branch of olive in his lips:

'At last, here is
Word of my word,
Breath of my breath,
Life of my life.'

And breeze and breath whispered back:
'This is he, this is he.'

Herod's Song

Twinkle, twinkle little star,
Now I wonder where you are.
Son of David born to be,
King, they say, instead of me.
We shall see, we shall see.

Little Lamb

Mary had a little lamb
His heart was pure as snow
And though he loved us very much
We told him where to go.

Christmas '94 — Bihac

Had they been Jews,
These hollowed out faces behind the twisted wire,
Had they been Jews we, who have seen
The footage, would have been sure to intervene.
But they lacked the telltale star.
So we did not know what it could mean
These hollowed out faces behind the twisted wire.

Had they been dolphins,
These blooded forms emerging from the smoke,
Had they been dolphins we, who have scanned
The papers, would have been sure to make a stand.
But they lacked the telltale nose.
So we did not know what it could mean
These blooded forms emerging from the smoke.

Had they been pheasants,
These bulleted bodies lying in the dirt,
Had they been pheasants we, who have been taught
Ethics, would have been sure to cry: this is not sport.
But they lacked the telltale feathers.
So we did not know what it could mean
These bulleted bodies lying in the dirt.

It is so difficult,
Wouldn't you agree,
Not to let difference
Blind us to similarity.

There

In the glimmer of a smile on a care-worn face
In the fountain fresh hope of a first embrace

There

When sun sparkles on the dancing foam
And laughter splashes like the hearts of home

There

In the pain and confusion and tears
The muffled screams and nameless fears

There

In the scuttling panic of a wind-whipped leaf
In the brimming ache of endless grief

There

In the emptiness of alone
In the grey barren of chilled stone

There

Always there

The eye brighter than the gleaming crown
The heart softer than the purple gown
The servant on the throne
The king who would be known

For no reason, except to give
In every season, that we might live.

Christmas Present

On this day
Give me this to give:

Some clue to speed a traveller's way
Some myrrh to sweeten death's decay
Some gold to feed a hungry child
Some word to bring us reconciled
Some balm to soothe an aching fear
Some smile to blossom through the year
Some hope to move the will to right
Some touch to give the shuttered sight
Some power to restrain the selfish knife
Some fragrance of that future life.

On this day
Give me this to give;
As you gave to me
And more.

Published by
Lion Publishing plc
Sandy Lane West, Oxford, England
ISBN 0 7459 3425 0

Albatross Books Pty Ltd
PO Box 320, Sutherland, NSW 2232, Australia
ISBN 0 7324 1408 3

First edition 1995

10 9 8 7 6 5 4 3 2 1 0